D1710839

United States Presidents

Gerald Ford

Paul Joseph
ABDO Publishing Company

visit us at
www.abdopub.com

Published by ABDO Publishing Company 4940 Viking Drive, Edina, Minnesota 55435.
Copyright © 2000 by Abdo Consulting Group, Inc. International copyrights reserved in all countries. No part of this book may be reproduced in any form without written permission from the publisher.

Printed in the United States.

Interior Photo credits: AP/Wide World, SuperStock, Archive, UPI/Corbis-Bettmann

Contributing editors: Robert Italia, Tamara L. Britton, K.M. Brielmaier, Kate A. Furlong

Library of Congress Cataloging-in-Publication Data

Joseph, Paul, 1970-
    Gerald Ford / Paul Joseph.
        p. cm. -- (United States presidents)
    Includes index.
    Summary: Presents details of the life and career of America's first appointed president.
    ISBN 1-57765-245-2
    1. Ford, Gerald, R., 1913- --Juvenile literature. 2. Presidents--United States--Biography --Juvenile literature. [1. Ford, Gerald R., 1913- . 2. Presidents.] I. Title. II. Series: United States presidents (Edina, Minn.)
E866.J67   1999
973.925'092--dc21
    [B]   98-6607
                                                             CIP
                                                              AC

Contents

Gerald Ford

*O*n August 9, 1974, Gerald Ford became president. He is the only person to hold the offices of president and vice president without being elected.

In 1972, President Richard Nixon and Vice President Spiro Agnew were re-elected. But Agnew had taken **bribes**. And he had cheated on his income taxes. He was forced to quit.

President Nixon chose Congressman Gerald Ford to replace Agnew. Less than a year later, the **Watergate scandal** forced President Nixon to quit. Gerald Ford became president.

"Our long national nightmare is over," Ford said to the American people after taking the oath of office. His leadership helped improve the economy. And he brought pride back to America after Watergate.

Gerald Ford

Gerald R. Ford (1913-)
Thirty-eighth President

BORN:	July 14, 1913 (named Leslie King at birth)
PLACE OF BIRTH:	Omaha, Nebraska
ANCESTRY:	Scots-English
FATHER:	Leslie King (1882-1941)
STEPFATHER:	Gerald R. Ford, Sr. (1890-1962) (Mother's second husband legally adopted her son in 1918, changing his name to Gerald R. Ford)
MOTHER:	Dorothy Gardner (1892-1967)
WIFE:	Elizabeth Bloomer (1918-)
CHILDREN:	Four: 3 boys, 1 girl
EDUCATION:	South High School, University of Michigan, Yale University Law School
RELIGION:	Episcopalian
OCCUPATION:	Lawyer
MILITARY SERVICE:	Enlisted as ensign in U.S. Naval Reserve, discharged as lieutenant commander (active duty 1942-1946)

POLITICAL PARTY: Republican

OFFICES HELD: Member of U.S. House of Representatives, minority leader in U.S. House of Representatives, vice president

AGE AT INAUGURATION: 61

YEARS SERVED: 1974-1977

VICE PRESIDENT: Nelson A. Rockefeller

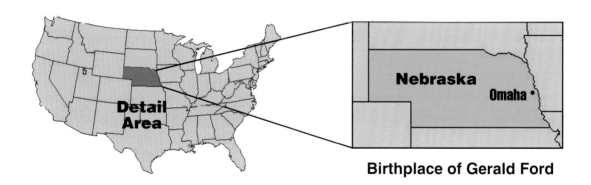

Birthplace of Gerald Ford

Young Jerry

Gerald Ford, Jr., was born on July 14, 1913, in Omaha, Nebraska. He was named Leslie King, Jr., after his father. But soon, his mother, Dorothy, divorced Leslie. Dorothy and Leslie, Jr., moved to Grand Rapids, Michigan.

In 1916, Dorothy married Gerald Ford. He owned a paint store. He was a respected community leader. Mr. Ford adopted Leslie, Jr., and gave him his name. Now, Leslie King, Jr., was Gerald Ford, Jr. He went by Jerry.

The Fords had three more children, Thomas, Richard, and James. They were a happy and loving family.

In 1929, the **Great Depression** began. Mr. Ford struggled to keep the paint store in business. Jerry helped make extra money by waiting tables and washing dishes at a restaurant.

In high school, Jerry was an excellent student. And he was on the football team. He played so well that he was voted to the All-State team. Jerry graduated in 1931.

Gerald Ford (circled) on his high school football team in 1930

Michigan and Yale

*J*erry received a scholarship from the University of Michigan. He played center on Michigan's undefeated national championship football teams of 1932 and 1933.

In 1934, Jerry was voted the team's most valuable player. In 1935, he was selected All-American as one of the best players in college football. Jerry also worked hard on his studies. He graduated near the top of his class in 1935.

The National Football League's Green Bay Packers and Detroit Lions wanted Jerry to play for them. But Jerry decided to coach sports and become a lawyer.

From 1935 to 1940, Jerry coached football and boxing at Yale University. In 1938, he started law school at Yale. There, Jerry worked for Wendell Willkie's 1940 presidential campaign. Franklin D. Roosevelt beat Willkie in the election. But Jerry had learned much about politics. He graduated from law school in 1941.

Ford returned to Grand Rapids. He opened a law firm with a friend. In 1941, the United States entered **World War II**. Ford joined the navy in 1942.

Ford worked as an athletic training officer for a year. Then he was transferred to the naval carrier USS *Monterey*. Ford served nearly four years in the navy. He rose to the rank of **lieutenant commander**, and earned many honors.

Ford returned home in 1946 to continue his law practice. He was interested in politics. His war experience made him think about America's role in the world and what he could do to help.

Gerald Ford played center for the University of Michigan football team.

Politics and Family

Gerald Ford decided to run for the **House of Representatives**. He got involved in the Red Cross, the United Way, and the Boy Scouts. He talked to people about their daily lives. They could see that Ford cared about them and their community.

Ford's opponent, Congressman Frank McKay, did not listen to the people like Ford did. Ford was elected in a landslide on November 2, 1948. Ford later said, "From that first day on, I knew I wanted the House to be my career."

Only two weeks before, Ford had married Elizabeth Ann Bloomer. She went by Betty. Betty was born in Chicago on April 8, 1918. She lived most of her life in Grand Rapids. As a young woman, she studied dance in New York City. Later, she returned to Grand Rapids and worked in a department store.

The Fords had three sons and a daughter. Michael was born in 1950. John was born in 1952. Steven was born in 1956, and Susan was born in 1957.

Congressman Ford studied the ways of **Congress**. He followed **debates**, learned how to get laws passed, and got ideas from the people he represented. Ford listened to his opponents and compromised with them. His abilities made him a popular congressman.

The members of the Ford family pictured on the White House grounds. From left, standing: Steve, Susan, Jack, Michael's wife Gayle, and Michael. The president and the first lady are seated.

Congressman Ford

*I*n **Congress**, Ford voted against expanding the power of the national government. He voted to limit **labor union** power. And he voted against minimum wage increases. Ford supported the **Civil Rights Act** of 1964. And he supported the **Voting Rights Act** of 1965.

Michigan voters liked Ford's actions in Congress. They re-elected him thirteen times with huge victories.

In 1951, Ford was elected to the House Appropriations Committee. This group of representatives decides how to spend tax money. Ford was on the Committee until 1965.

In 1963, President John F. Kennedy was **assassinated**. Ford served as a member of the Warren Commission. This group investigated the assassination. They decided that Lee

Lee Harvey Oswald

14

Harvey Oswald shot President Kennedy. In 1965, Ford wrote a book about Oswald. He called it *Portrait of the Assassin.*

In 1965, the **Republicans** voted Ford the minority leader in the **House of Representatives**. At the time, there were more **Democrats** than Republicans in **Congress**. So the Republicans were in the minority. Gerald Ford was their leader.

Ford attended most sessions of Congress. He also averaged nearly 200 out-of-town speeches each year. In 1966, Ford's speeches helped get forty-seven Republicans elected to the House of Representatives.

In 1970, Ford attempted to **impeach** Supreme Court Justice William O. Douglas. Douglas had received money for work done outside the government. Ford felt this work was illegal. But the impeachment attempt failed. Ford's good name in Congress suffered. But he soon recovered.

Ford wanted to become the **Speaker of the House**. To do that, there had to be more Republicans than Democrats in the House. But the Republicans could not win the majority. Ford decided that the 1974 election would be his last. Then he would retire.

The Making of the Thirty-eighth United States President

1913	**1916**	**1932**	**1934**
Born Leslie King, Jr., in Omaha, Nebraska, on July 14	Mother Dorothy marries Gerald R. Ford who adopts Leslie, Jr., and changes his name	Plays center on the University of Michigan football team	Named Most Valuable Player of Michigan football team

1941	**1942**	**1948**	**1950**
Graduates from law school	Joins navy; serves in World War II	Marries Elizabeth Ann "Betty" Bloomer; elected to House of Representatives	Son Michael is born

1957	**1963**	**1965**	**1973**
Daughter Susan is born	Member of the Warren Commission	Voted House minority leader	Replaces Spiro Agnew as vice president

Gerald Ford

"My fellow Americans, our long national nightmare is over. Our Constitution works. Our great republic is a government of laws and not of men. Here, the people rule . . ."

1935
Graduates from college; named All-American

1935
Begins coaching football and boxing at Yale University

1938
Begins law school at Yale

Historic Events
during Ford's Presidency

First successful landing on Mars by *Viking I*

Frank Robinson of Cleveland Indians becomes first African American manager in major league baseball

United States celebrates its 200th birthday on July 4, 1976

1951
Member of the House Appropriations Committee through 1965

1952
Son John is born

1956
Son Steven is born

1974
President Nixon resigns; Ford becomes president, pardons Nixon

1975
Two assassination attempts on Ford's life in September

1976
Jimmy Carter is elected President

1977
Ford retires to California

1980
Ford is asked to run as Reagan's vice president, he says no

PRESIDENTIAL YEARS

An Appointed President

*O*n October 10, 1973, Vice President Spiro Agnew quit his job. He had taken **bribes** and lied on his income taxes. President Nixon had to pick a new vice president.

Nixon wanted someone with similar political views. He wanted his new vice president to be loyal. And the new vice president had to be good enough to one day be elected president. Nixon thought Ford was the best choice.

The U.S. Senate approved of Ford as the vice president. He was sworn into office on December 6, 1973. It was the first time in U.S. history that a vice president had been appointed.

Within months, a **scandal** known as **Watergate** began to surface. Burglars had broken into the main office of the **Democratic** party at the Watergate Complex in Washington, D.C. They wanted information about the Democratic Party. The burglars worked for President Nixon. He tried to cover up his involvement, but failed.

President Nixon was forced to quit his office. On August 9, 1974, Gerald Ford became the first president in U.S. history who was not elected by the people.

Ford called on all Americans to try to move past **Watergate**. "Our long national nightmare is over," he said. "Our Constitution works. Our great republic is a government of laws and not of men." He promised to work with both **Democrats** and **Republicans** to get the country back to normal.

President Richard Nixon (front) makes a speech before Congress while Vice President Ford listens.

The Thirty-eighth President

*O*n September 8, 1974, President Ford **pardoned** Richard Nixon for "all offenses against the United States which he . . . has committed or may have committed or taken part in." This meant that Nixon could never be sent to jail for his **Watergate** crimes.

President Ford believed that pardoning Nixon would help the country move on. But Nixon's pardon angered most Americans. They believed that no one was above the law, not even the president. They wanted Nixon punished for what he had done. After the pardon, Ford's popularity dropped.

Americans were also unhappy with Ford's next decision. Many young men did not want to fight in the **Vietnam War**. They left the country and deserted the army. Ford decided to let them come back. But they had to do government service for two years.

Some people thought these young men deserved worse punishment. Others wanted Ford to **pardon** them.

On December 19, 1974, President Ford chose New York governor Nelson A. Rockefeller as the new vice president. For the first time in its history, America had a president and a vice president who were not elected into office.

President Ford quickly turned his attention to the economy. Many people were out of work. Prices for goods and services were rising fast. The country had a shortage of oil and gas.

President Ford (right) with Vice President Nelson Rockefeller

President Ford worked hard on the economy. He agreed to cut taxes. And he held down government spending. By May 1975, more Americans went back to work. Business improved.

At the same time, the **Vietnam War** was ending. In March 1975, Ford ordered the last American troops out of Vietnam. Americans were relieved that the war was over.

On May 12, 1975, the S.S. *Mayaguez*, a merchant ship, was seized off the Cambodian coast. Thirty-nine Americans were captured. Ford wanted to keep merchant shipping safe. He also knew that America needed to look strong after the Vietnam War. Ford sent in the U.S. Marines, and the crew was rescued.

On September 6, 1975, Ford was in California to give a speech. On his way to Governor Jerry Brown's office, Ford saw a woman in the crowd point a gun at him. The woman, Lynette "Squeaky" Fromme, was arrested before she shot the president. She was sentenced to life in prison.

On September 22, Ford was back in California to speak at a labor meeting. Outside a San Francisco hotel, Sarah Jane

Moore shot at him. Ford was not hurt and Moore was caught. She also was sentenced to life in prison.

Ford began to prepare for the 1976 presidential election. He hoped that Americans would give him a chance to continue leading the country. President Ford believed that he needed another term to fix America's problems.

President Ford (center) ducks behind his limousine after a shot was fired as he left the St. Francis Hotel in San Francisco, California.

The Seven "Hats" of the U.S. President

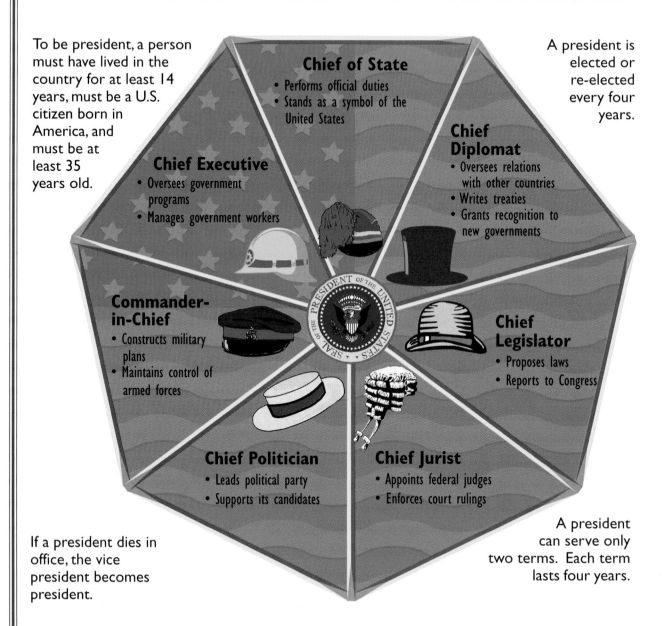

To be president, a person must have lived in the country for at least 14 years, must be a U.S. citizen born in America, and must be at least 35 years old.

A president is elected or re-elected every four years.

Chief of State
- Performs official duties
- Stands as a symbol of the United States

Chief Diplomat
- Oversees relations with other countries
- Writes treaties
- Grants recognition to new governments

Chief Executive
- Oversees government programs
- Manages government workers

Commander-in-Chief
- Constructs military plans
- Maintains control of armed forces

Chief Legislator
- Proposes laws
- Reports to Congress

Chief Politician
- Leads political party
- Supports its candidates

Chief Jurist
- Appoints federal judges
- Enforces court rulings

If a president dies in office, the vice president becomes president.

A president can serve only two terms. Each term lasts four years.

As president, Gerald Ford had seven jobs.

The Three Branches of the U.S. Government

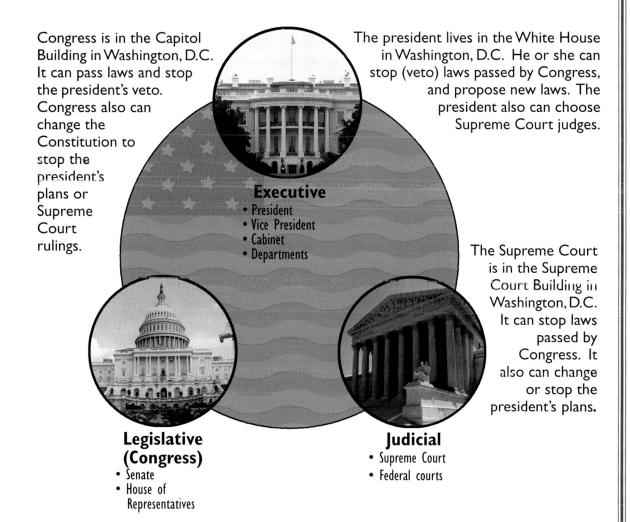

Congress is in the Capitol Building in Washington, D.C. It can pass laws and stop the president's veto. Congress also can change the Constitution to stop the president's plans or Supreme Court rulings.

The president lives in the White House in Washington, D.C. He or she can stop (veto) laws passed by Congress, and propose new laws. The president also can choose Supreme Court judges.

Executive
- President
- Vice President
- Cabinet
- Departments

The Supreme Court is in the Supreme Court Building in Washington, D.C. It can stop laws passed by Congress. It also can change or stop the president's plans.

Legislative (Congress)
- Senate
- House of Representatives

Judicial
- Supreme Court
- Federal courts

The U.S. Constitution formed three government branches. Each branch has power over the others. So, no single group or person can control the country. The Constitution calls this "separation of powers."

After the White House

*P*resident Ford campaigned very hard for president in 1976. He chose Senator Bob Dole of Kansas to be his vice president. The **Democrats** chose Jimmy Carter to run for president. Ford lost a very close election.

In his first speech as president, Carter said, "For myself and for our nation, I want to thank [Gerald Ford] for all he has done to heal our land." Most Americans agreed with the new president. Ford became president during one of the worst times in American history and did an honorable job.

The Fords retired to Rancho Mirage, California. Gerald Ford became highly respected after he left the White House. Ronald Reagan asked him to be his vice presidential running mate in 1980. Ford said no, but continued to work for the **Republican** party. He gave speeches and raised money.

Gerald Ford will be remembered as the only president in history not elected by the people. But he should be remembered for much more. Gerald Ford brought honor and pride back to the White House.

President Ford with Senator Bob Dole (left)

Fun Facts

- Ford was the only president who once worked as a male model. He appeared in *Look* magazine.

- Gerald Ford once won a trip to Washington, D.C., in a contest run by a local movie theater as the "most popular high school senior."

- President Ford's favorite lunch was cottage cheese smothered in catsup.

- Ford needed only four hours of sleep a night.

- On the day of his wedding, Ford was reported to have been so nervous that he showed up with one brown shoe and one black.

- President Ford took his dog out for a walk around the White House one night and locked himself out. After about 45 minutes a guard finally let him in. Ford was in his bathrobe and slippers!

- Betty Ford had a CB radio in the White House. She liked to talk to truckers who were passing through Washington, D.C. Her "handle" was First Mama.

Betty and Gerald Ford

Glossary

assassinate - to murder a very important person.

bribe - anything given to someone so they will do something wrong, dishonest, or illegal.

Civil Rights Act - act that stopped discrimination based on race, religion, or national origin. It was passed in 1964.

Congress - the lawmaking body of a nation. It is made up of the Senate and the House of Representatives.

debate - to discuss a question or topic.

Democrat - one of the two main political parties in the United States. Democrats are often more liberal and believe in more government.

Great Depression - the failure of the U.S. economy starting in 1929 and lasting through the 1930s. A depression is a time when business is slow and people are out of work.

House of Representatives - a group of people elected by citizens to represent them. They meet in Washington, D.C., and make laws for the country.

impeach - to have a trial to decide if an elected official should be removed from office.

labor union - a group formed to help workers receive their rights.

lieutenant commander - a naval rank above lieutenant and below commander.

pardon - to forgive anything illegal that a person has done. When a person is pardoned they never have to stand trial or go to jail.

Republican - one of two main political parties in the United States. Republicans are often more conservative and believe in less government.

scandal - a shameful act that brings disgrace or shocks the public.

Speaker of the House - the highest ranking congressman in the party that has the majority.

Vietnam War - 1955-1975. A long, failed attempt by the U.S. to help keep South Vietnam from being taken over by North Vietnam.

Voting Rights Act - act that removed all barriers meant to keep African Americans from voting, such as literacy tests and poll taxes.

Watergate - a 1972 political crime involving President Nixon's administration. Nixon's people broke into the Watergate Complex and tried to steal information about the Democrats. The burglars were caught and sent to jail. Nixon was forced to quit.

World War II - 1939 to 1945, fought in Europe, Asia, and Africa. The United States, France, Great Britain, the Soviet Union, and their allies were on one side; Germany, Italy, Japan, and their allies were on the other side. The war began when Germany invaded Poland. America entered the war in 1941 after Japan bombed Pearl Harbor, Hawaii.

Internet Sites

United States Presidents Information Page
http://historyoftheworld.com/soquel/prez.htm
Links to information about United States presidents. This site is very informative, with biographies on every president as well as speeches and debates, and other links.

The Presidents of the United States of America
http://www.whitehouse.gov/WH/glimpse/presidents/html/presidents.html
This site is from the White House. With an introduction from President Bill Clinton and biographies that include each president's inaugural address, this site is excellent. Get information on White House history, art in the White House, first ladies, first families, and much more.

POTUS—Presidents of the United States
http://www.ipl.org/ref/POTUS/
In this resource you will find background information, election results, cabinet members, presidency highlights, and some odd facts on each of the presidents. Links to biographies, historical documents, audio and video files, and other presidential sites are also included to enrich this site.

These sites are subject to change. Go to your favorite search engine and type in United States presidents for more sites.

Pass It On

History enthusiasts: educate readers around the country by passing on information you've learned about presidents or other important people who've changed history. Share your little-known facts and interesting stories. We want to hear from you!

To get posted on the ABDO Publishing Company Web site, email us at:
history@abdopub.com
Visit the ABDO Publishing Company Web site at www.abdopub.com

Index